# HOW TO DRAW EVERYTHING

## FOR KIDS

**ages 4-8**

# 300

## CUTE STEP-BY-STEP DRAWINGS STUFF

OF_____

# WONDERS
# FASCINATING

Rainbow
House
Raccoon
Unicorn
Watering Can
Dress
Snowman
Beaver Devil
Christmas tree
Gnome
Traffic Light
Cinderella
Clock
Star
Retro TV
Hair clip
Paper bag
Notebook
Pencil
Light bulb
Potion
High heel
Pencil
Ghost
Screwdriver
Band-aid
Socks
Suitcase
Bag
Wallet
Rainbow
Eraser
Teeth

Soap
Dumpling
Drill
Snow White
Hammer
Stapler
Phone
Pin
Mermaid
Eye shadow
Crayon
Mirror
Marker
Sleeping mask
Heart box
Tablet
Book
Tornado
Letter
Heart jar
Aurora
Kawaii Drop
Bubble
Teeth
Shoe
Sun
Bat
Face wash
Book
Easter egg
Brain
Plane
Skull

Sock
Dango
Nail polish
Heart
Glue
World
Fire
Record player
Thermometer
Perfume
Heart Message
Lipstick
Santa
Present box
Hairbrush
Umbrella
School palette
Shampoo
Magic wand
Bath puff
Potion bottles
Guitar
Stapler
Ghost
Cloud
Scissors
Backpack
Mermaid Tail
Toilet paper
Candle
Bathtub
Trophy
Hair dryer

# ANIMALS

Sloth
Bee
Cat
Narwhal
Turtle
Monkey
Dinosaur
Cow
Mouse
Octopus
Bear
Fish
Hippopotamus
Pig
Giraffe
Dragon
Koala
Pufferfish
Bone
Bird
Snail
Axolotl

Dinosaur
Elephant
Turtle
Seahorse
Butterfly
Beetle
squid
jellyfish
hamster
rabbit
whale
chick
rabbit
hamster
bear
starfish
seal
crab
squirrel
owl
platypus

Llama
Mouse
Hedgehog
Penguin
Rabbit
Shell
with pearl
Sheep
Dog
Sloth
Snail
Rabbit
Eggplant
Sharpener
Lion
Deer
Butterfly
Panda bear
Dog
Red panda

3

# PLANTS

Ball
Corn
Leaf
Cactus
Mobile star
toy
Ball
Bat and ball
Car
Stop sign Block
Tree
Durian
Baby bottle
Duck toy
Carriage
Motorbike
Pear
Avocado
Spaceship
Pliers
Pomegranate

Pacifier
Hot air balloon
Ship
Coconut
Train
Strawberry
Robot
Cucumber
Flower in vase
Coconut tree
Bus
Pineapple
Banana
Magic ball
Papaya
Carrot
Turnip
Ball
Toy
Pot

Onion
Watermelon
Orange
Mango
Shallots
Stop sign
block
Apple
Toy
Pear
Stone
Cherry
Mushroom
Aloe vera
Peach
Flower
Rocket
Bowling
Submarine
Boat
Plane

# KITCHEN AND DRINKS

Meat
Beetroot
Pumpkin
Candy
Beet
Tea Pot
Sausage
Star Apple
Shrimp Tempura
Hot Cocoa
Milk tea
Bread
Bottle
Kitchen
Scale
Paper bag
Pizza
Egg
Burrito
Chocolate

Popcorn
Sushi
French fries
Gingerbread
Avocado
Pineapple
Cup
Bread
Burger
Juice
Sushi
Chocolate
Bar
Sausages
Kitchen whisk
Grocery bag
Bread
Mug
Jello

Lollipop
Tea bottle
Coffee
Croissant
Ketchup
Chicken leg
Sauce
Sandwich
Cinnabon
Tea Pot
Blender
Sauce
Ice cream
Packaging
Milk
Bacon
Nigiri
Egg
Cupcake

## Raccoon

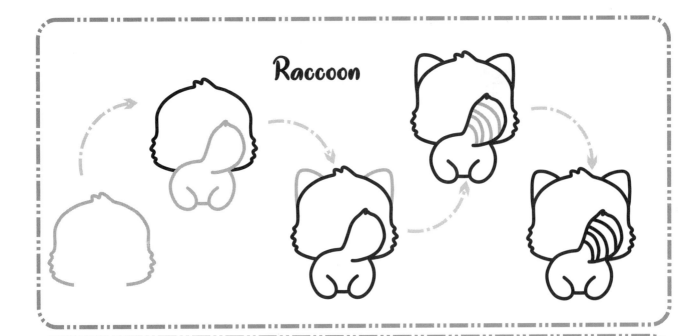

## Devil Beaver

## Bear

# Gnome

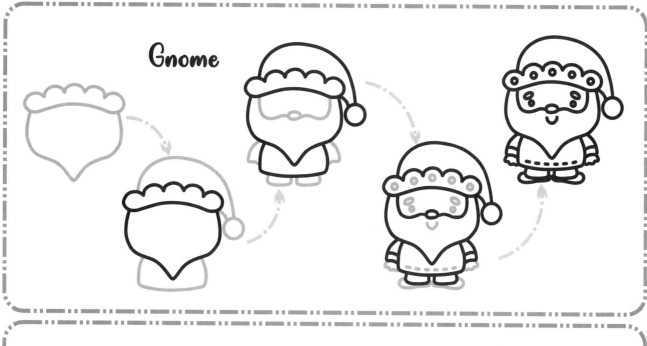

# Fish

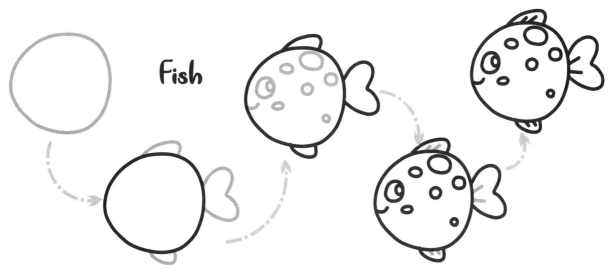

# Snowman

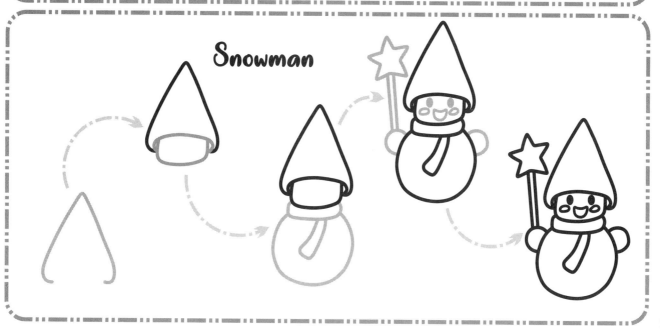

Aurora

kawaii leaf

Durián

# Christmas tree

# Coffee

# Croissant

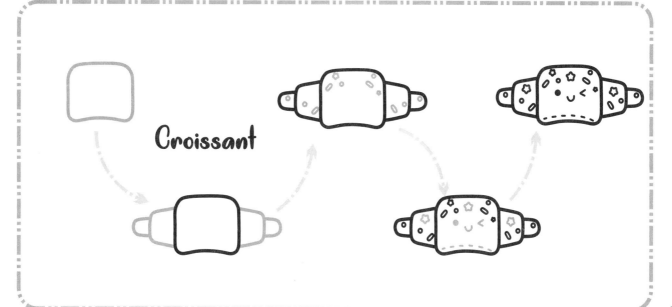

pineapple

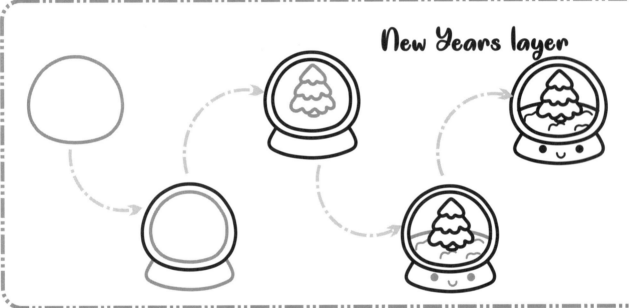

New Years layer

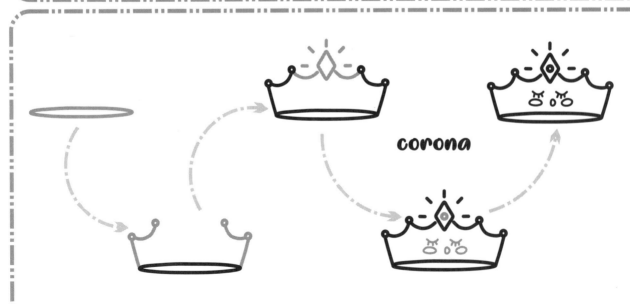

corona

# Avocado

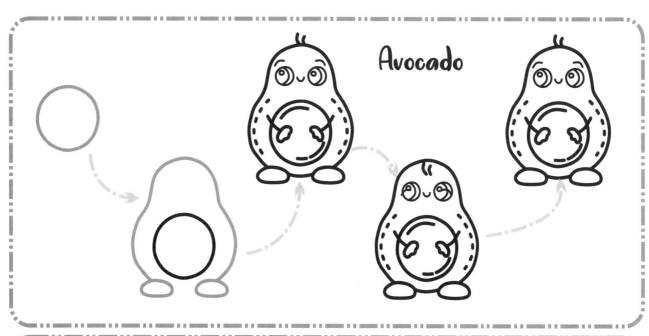

# Bat and ball

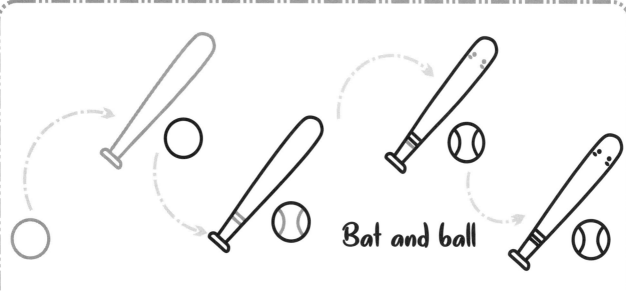

# Gingerbread

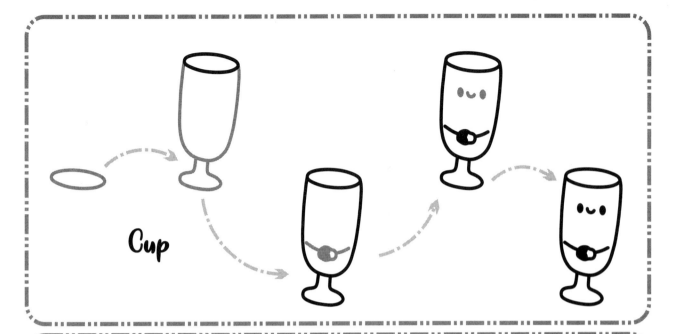

Cup

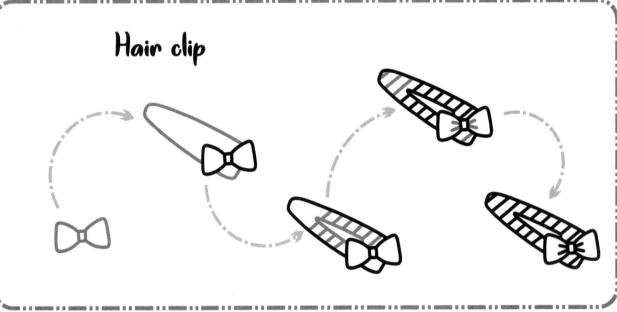

Hair clip

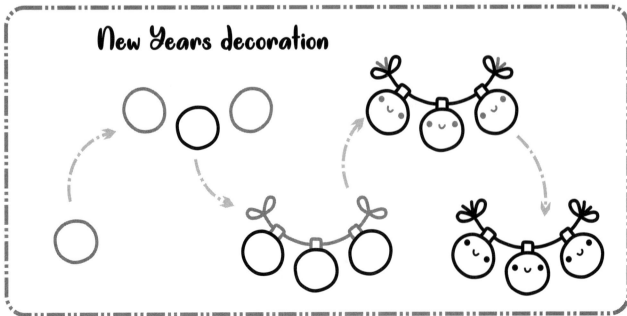

New Years decoration

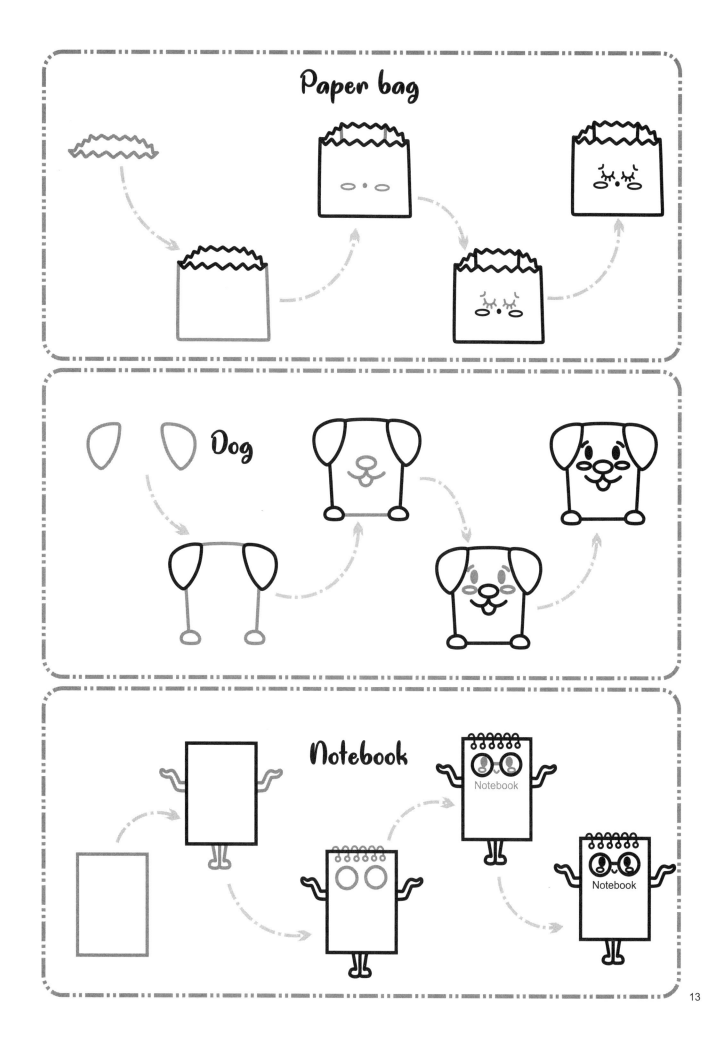

# Paper bag

# Dog

# Notebook

13

Car

Jellyfish

Hámster

14

# Dress

# Chicken thigh

# Sheep

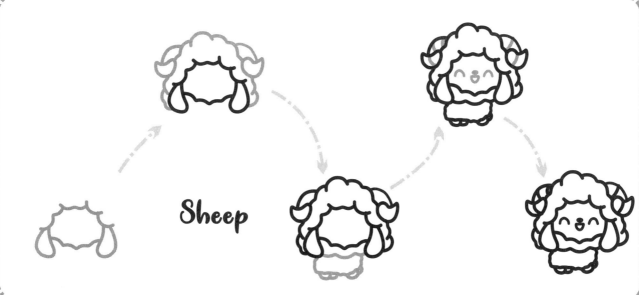

Ketchup

Shell
with pearl

star

Rabbit

Mobile star toy

Sea urchin

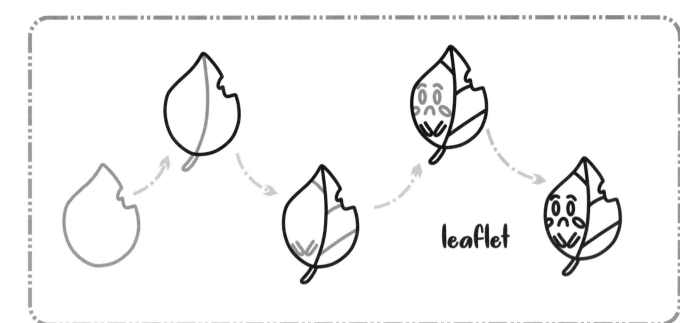

leaflet

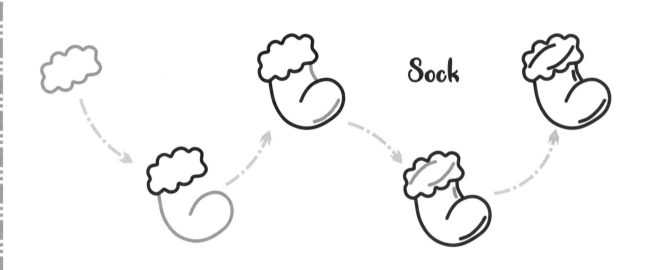

Sock

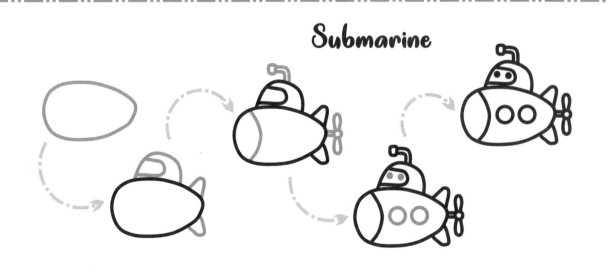

Submarine

bubble tea

Penguin

Mouse

19

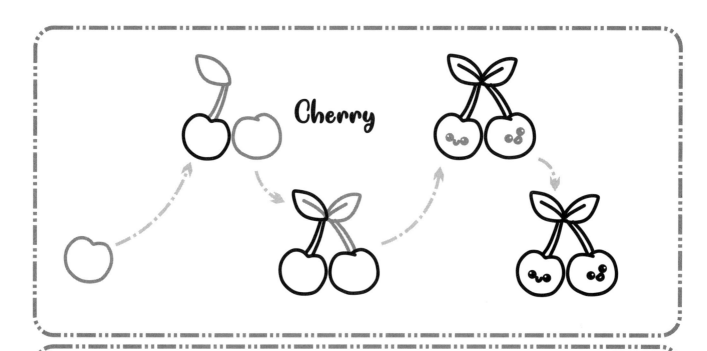

Cherry

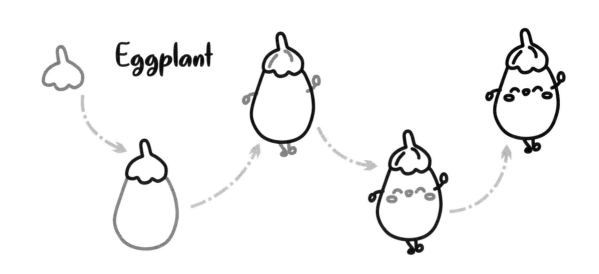

Eggplant

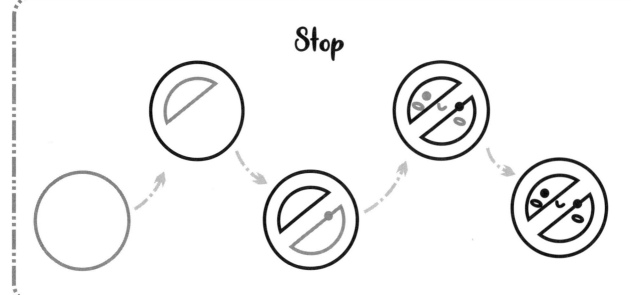

Stop

20

# Heart

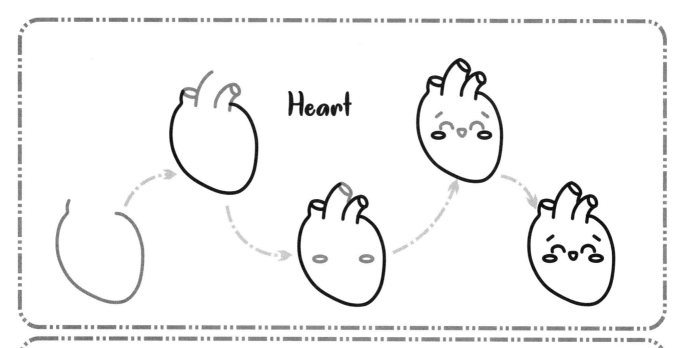

# Tree

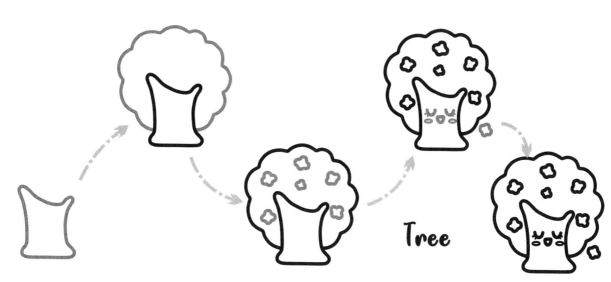

# Heart message

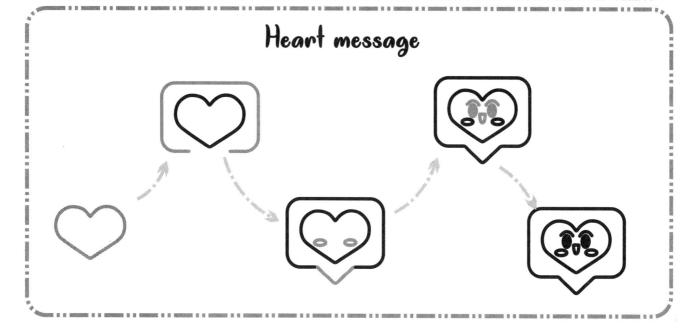

# Lightbulb

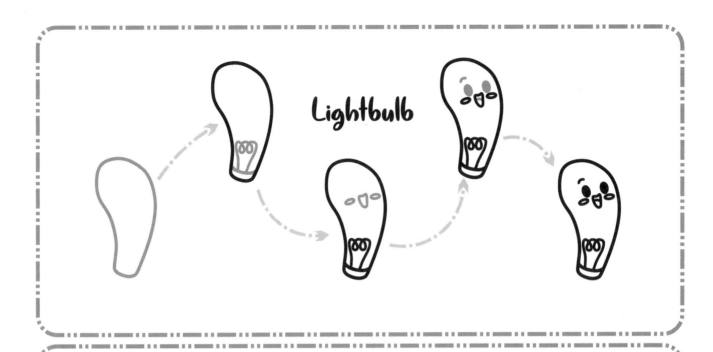

# High heel

# Band aid

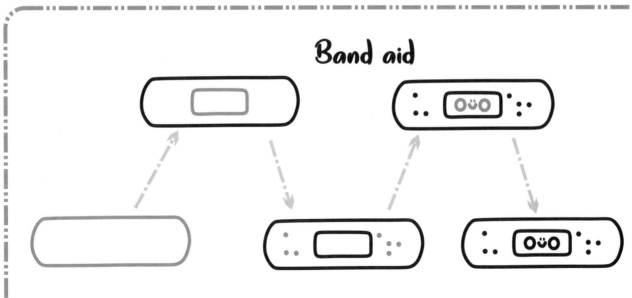

Hamburger

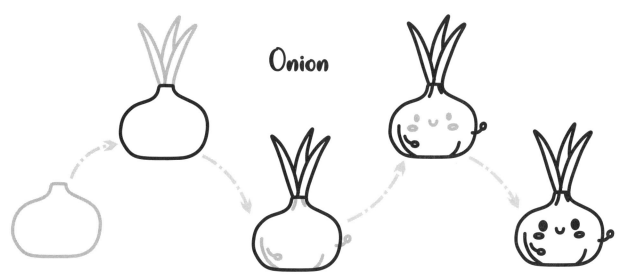

Onion

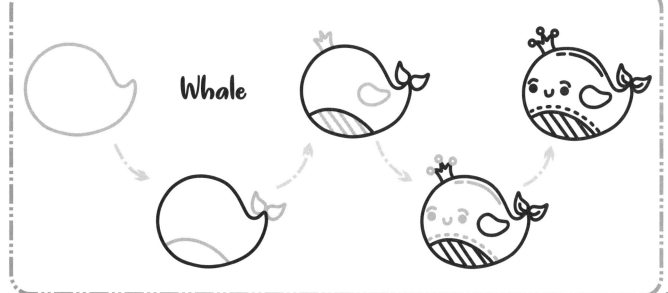

Whale

# Rabbit

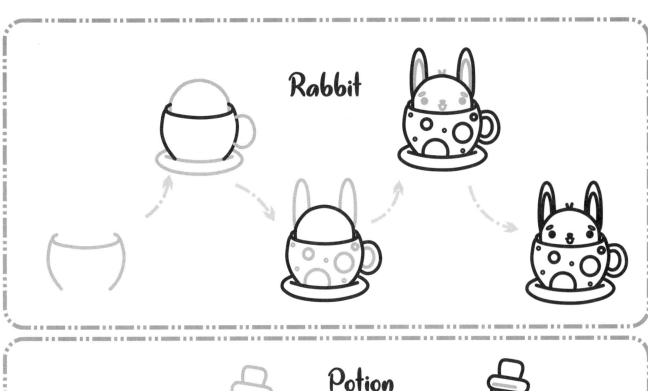

# Potion

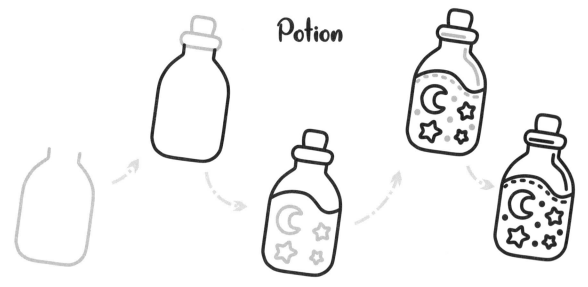

# Television

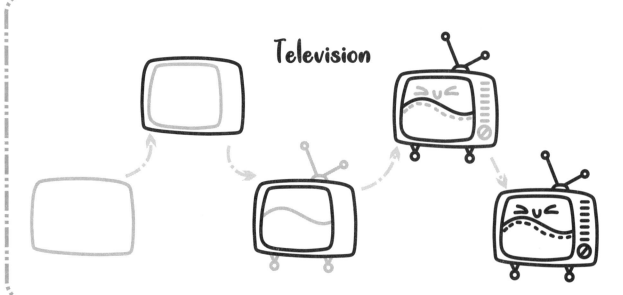

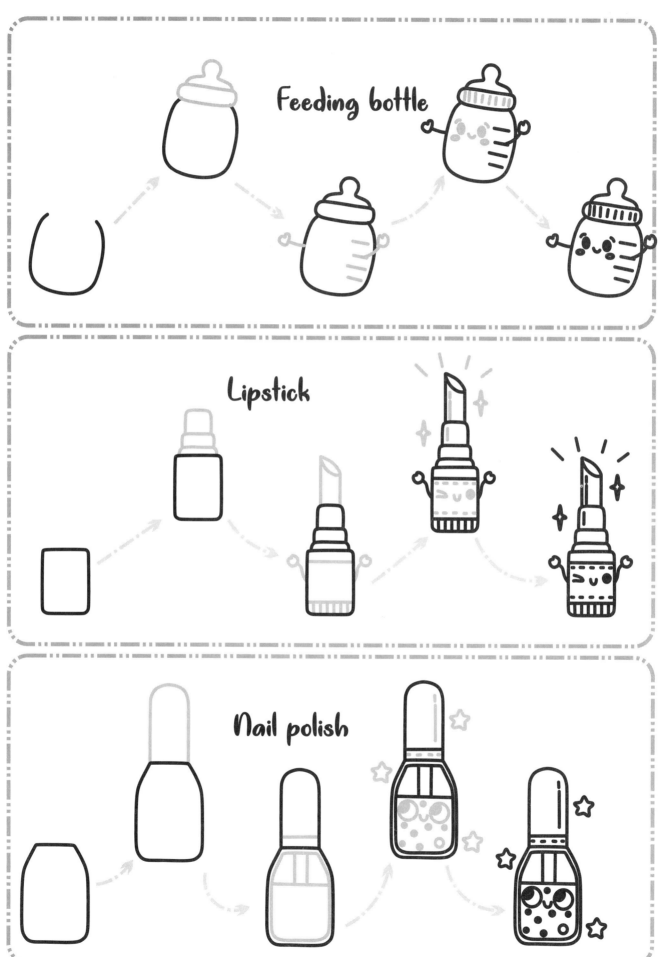

Feeding bottle

Lipstick

Nail polish

25

Socks

Rabbit

Toy

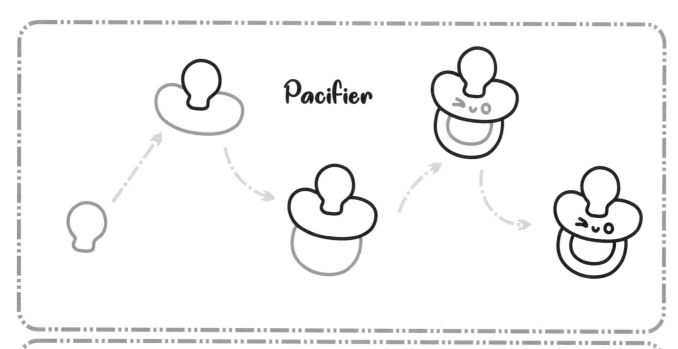

Pacifier

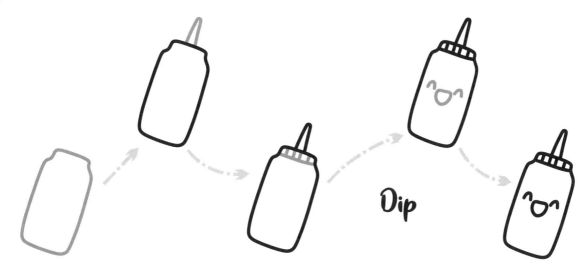

Dip

Kettle

Tea with milk

Kettle

candy

Home

Traffic light

Star apple

# Snail

# Lazy

# Gift box

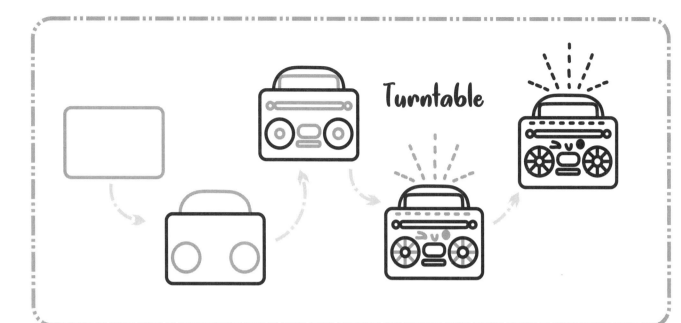

Turntable

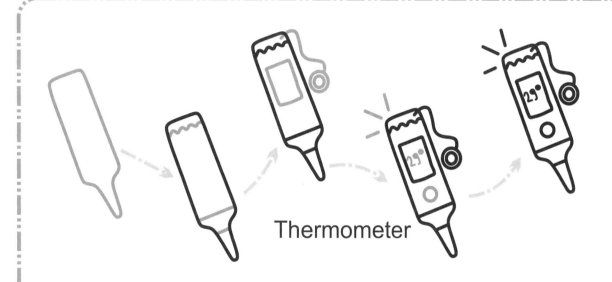

Thermometer

Perfume

31

Sushi

Umbrella

School palette

# Bread

# Blender

# Watermelon

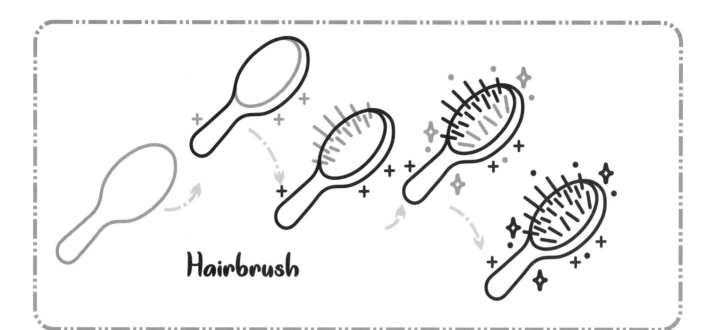

Hairbrush

Suitcase

Kitchen scale

Santa Claus

Bag

Orange

## Shampoo

## Wand

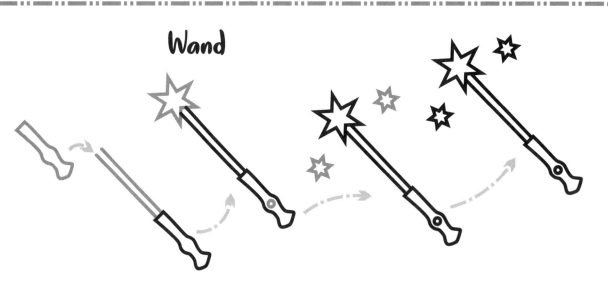

## Bath tassel

**Of juices**

**Train**

**Ship**

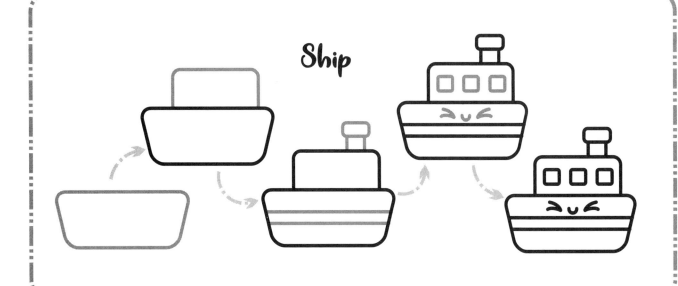

## Ghost

## chocolate

## Chick

## Dip

## Fan

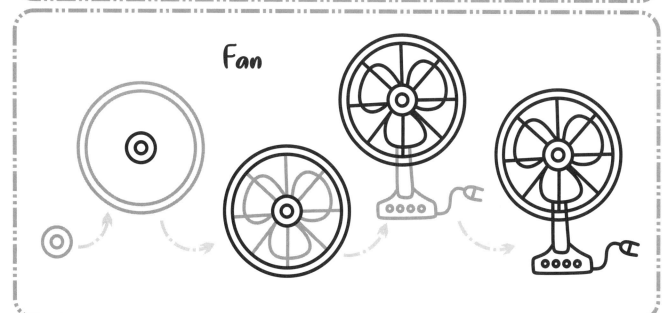

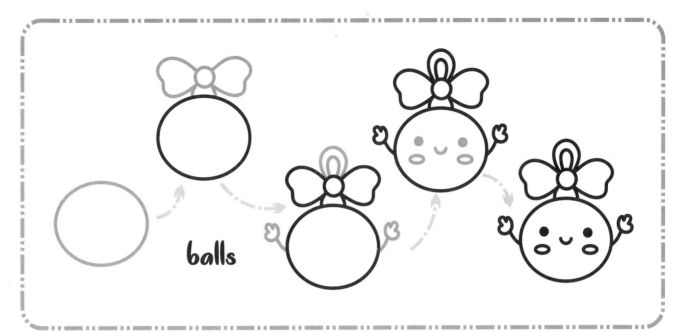

balls

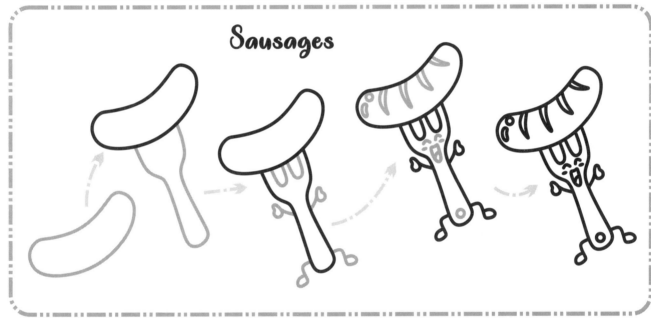

Sausages

Shrimp in tempura

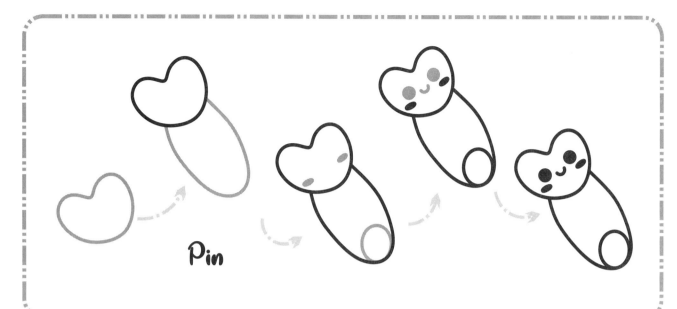

Pin

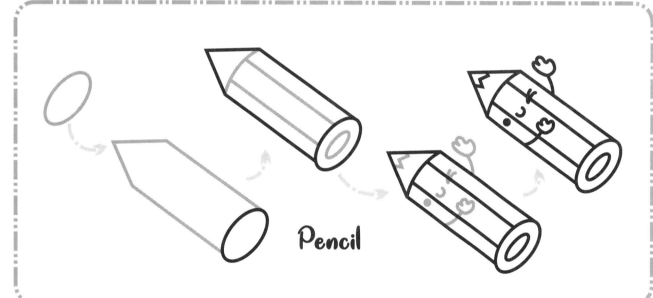

Pencil

Hot air pencil

## Flower in vase

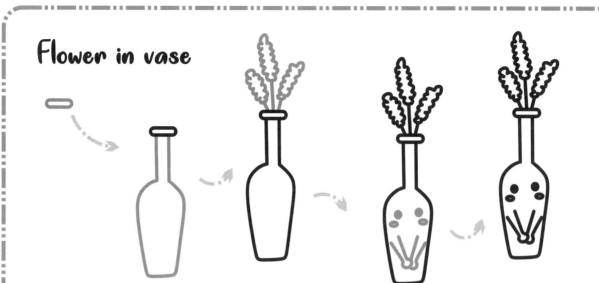

## Toy Duck

## Carriage

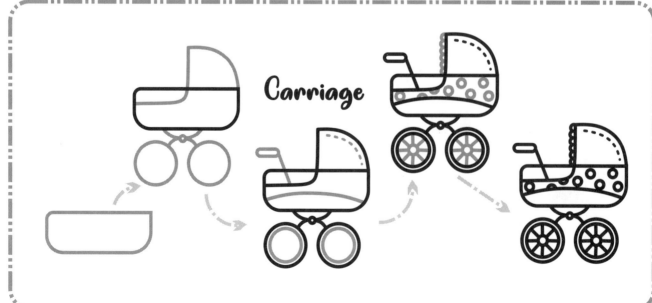

## Stapler

## Kitchen mixer

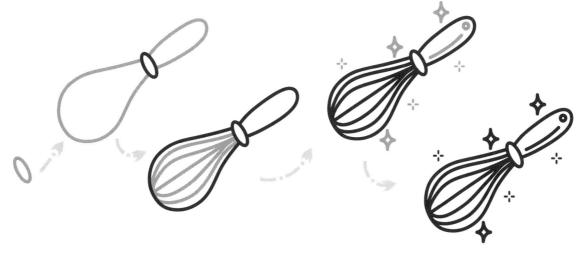

## Pencil Sharpener

Butterfly

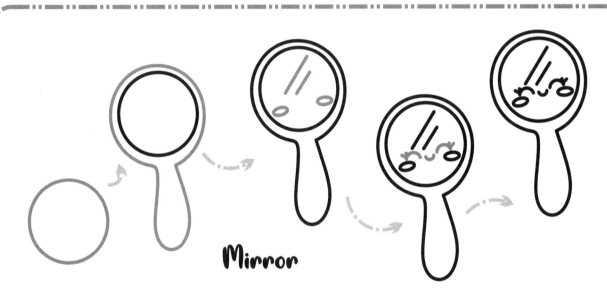

Mirror

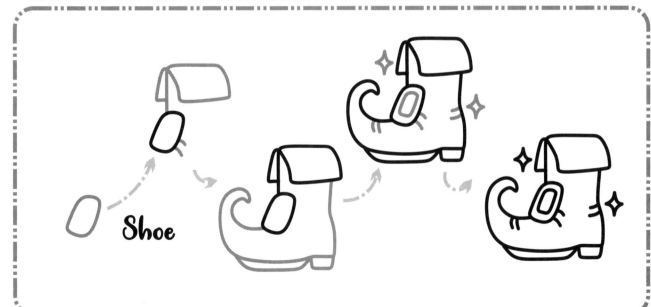

Shoe

44

# Toy

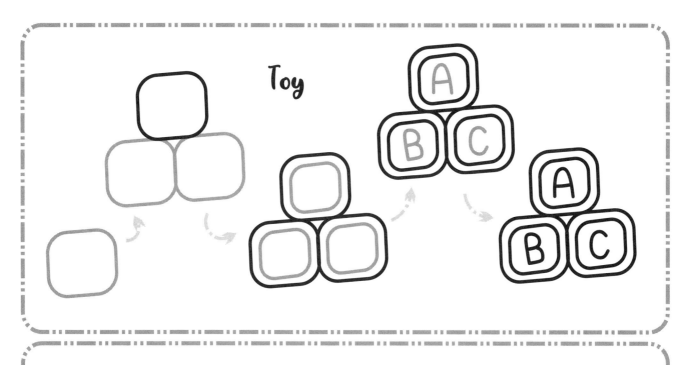

# Panda bear

# Robot

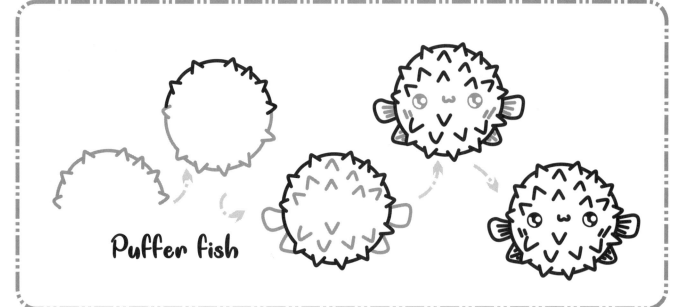

**Puffer fish**

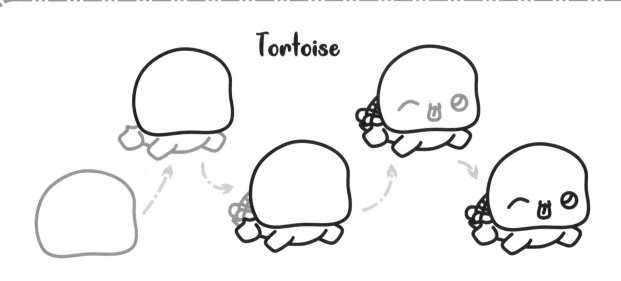

**Tortoise**

**Bun**

## Crab

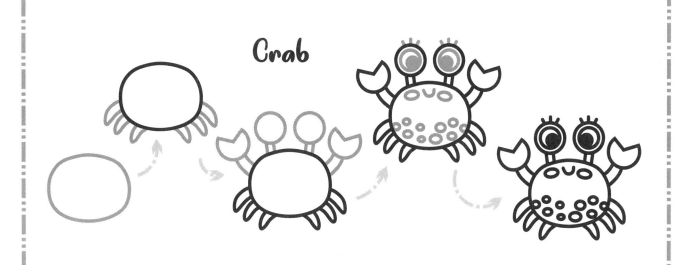

## Lion

## Seal

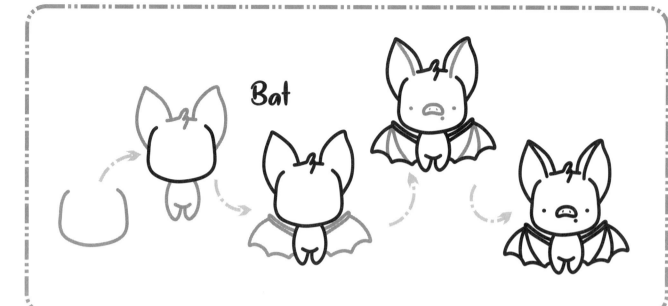

Bat

Shallots

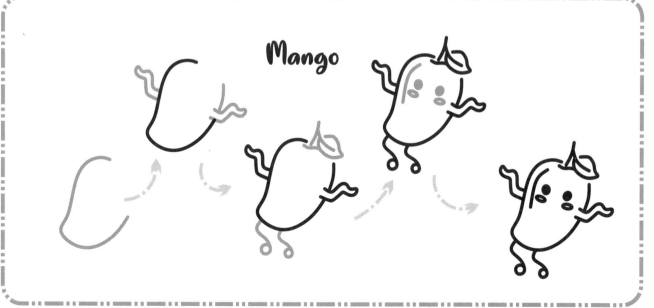

Mango

# Bacon

# Empanadillas

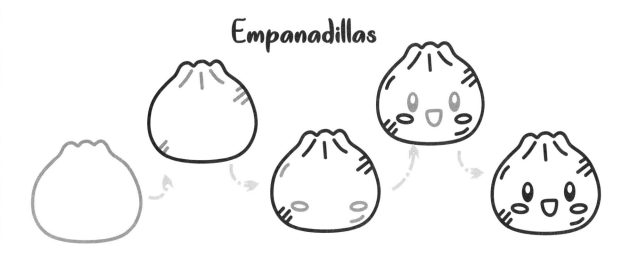

# Sausages

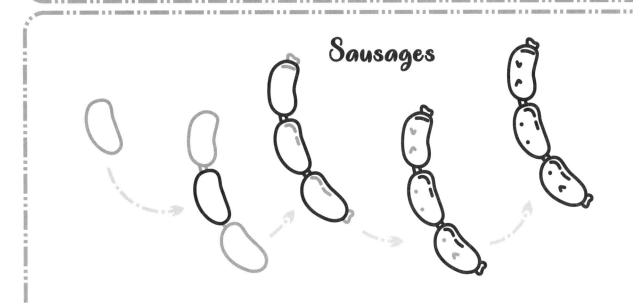

Hámster

Red panda

Bear

egg

Mouse

Hippo

## Starfish

## Snow White

## Coconut tree

# Motorbike

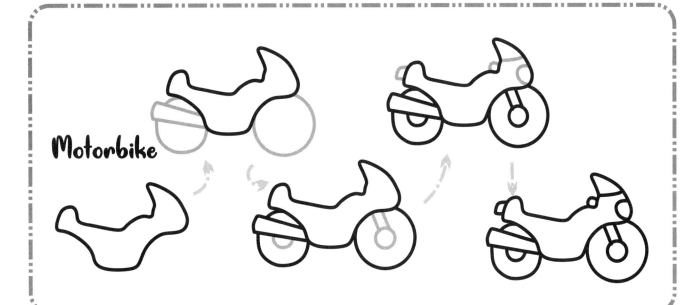

# Bus

# Heart box

# Bottle

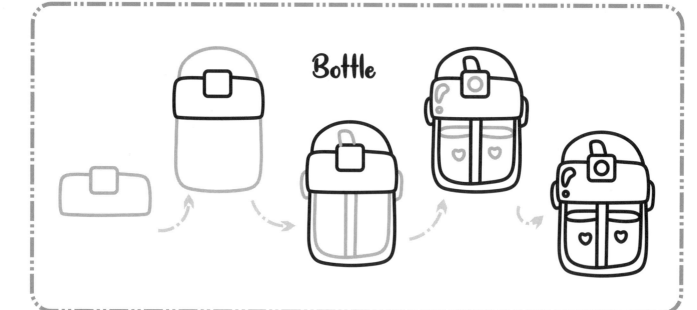

# Tablet

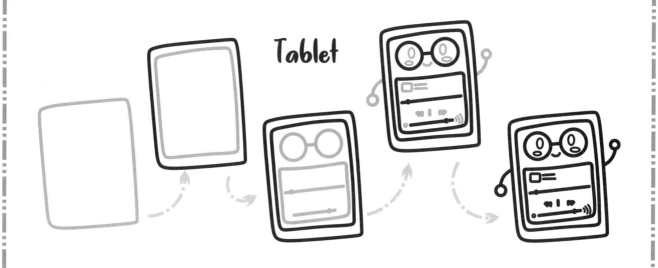

# Book

# Pear

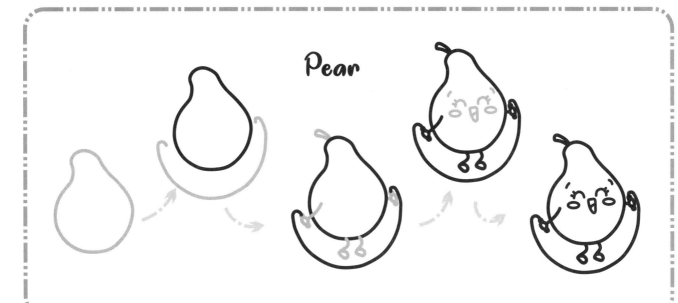

# Shopping bag

# Sun

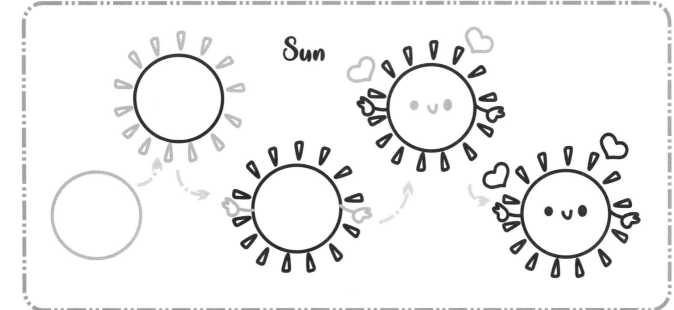

# Rainbow

# Teeth

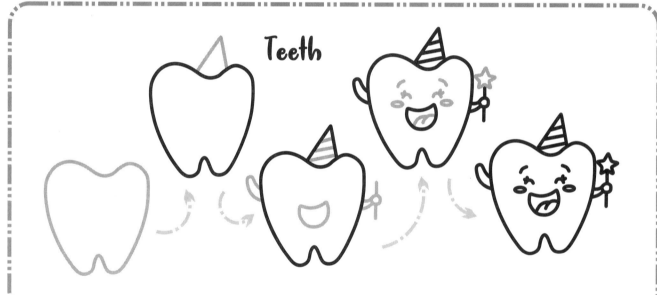

# Cucumber

# Egg

# Apple

# Bone

## Tornado

## Letter

## Heart shaped jar

# Pizza

# Stop singing

# ice cream

Dog

Sushi

Milk packaging

# Burrito

# Teeth

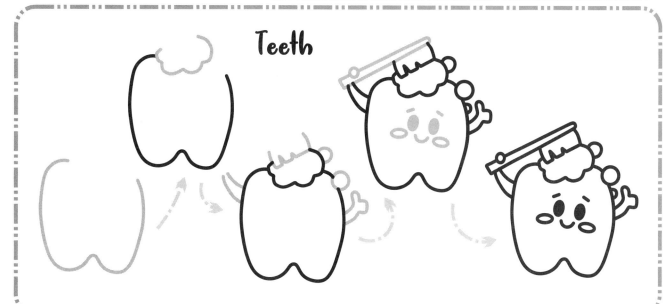

# Strawberry

## Watering can

## Cactus

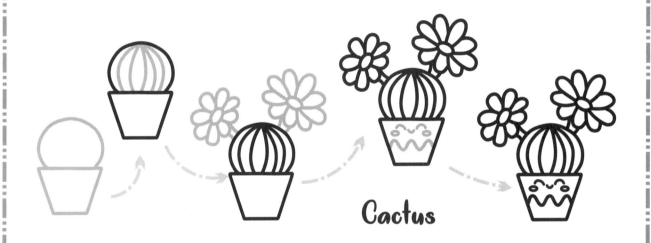

## Cinderella

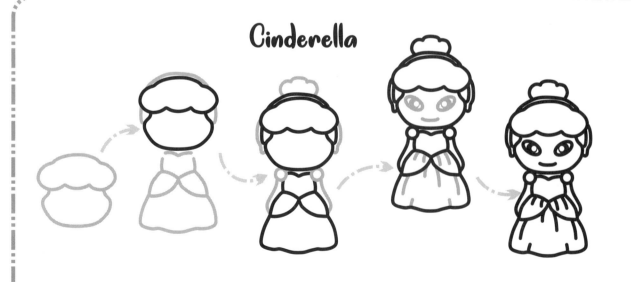

## Squirrel

## Paper bag

## Deer

Banana

axolotl

Cupcake

# Penguin

# Cloud

# Narwhal

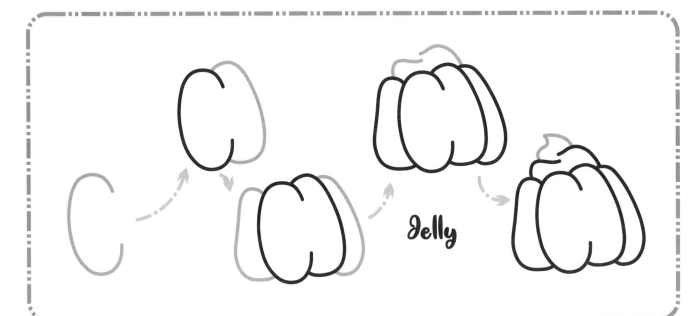

Jelly

Toilet paper

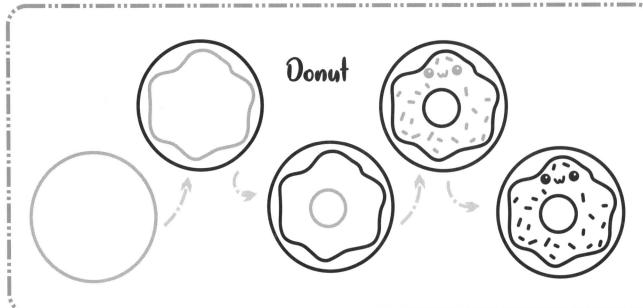

Donut

## Dinosaur

## Umbrella

## Hámster

# Squid

# Flower

# Butterfly

## Aloe vera

## Cat Avocado

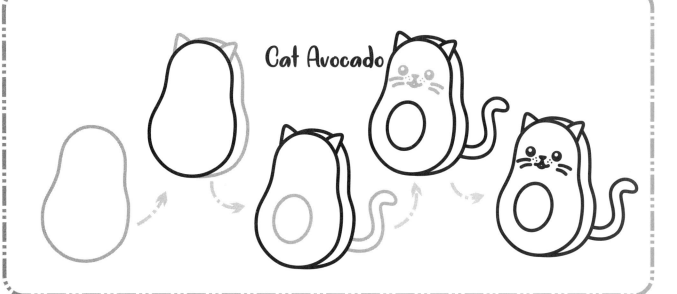

## Elephant

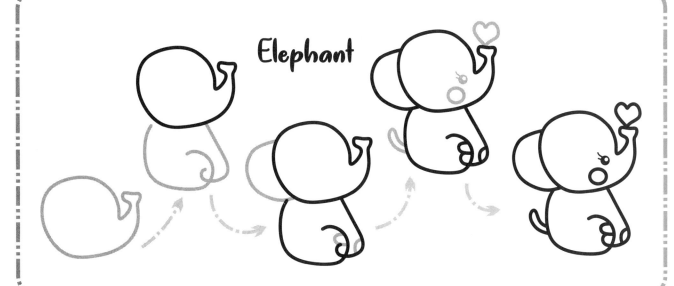

# Ghost

# Popcorn

# Juice

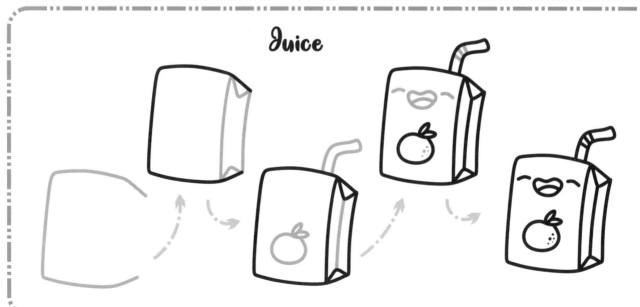

# Cool Bird

# Snail

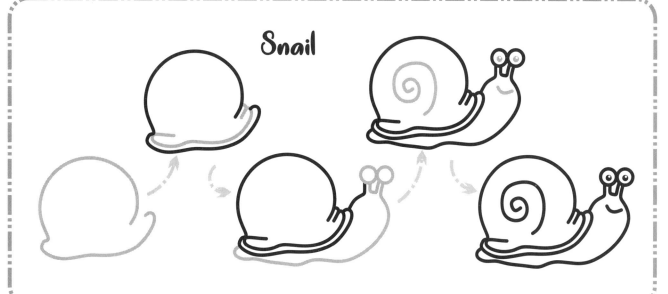

# Peach

## Pear

## Chocolate

## Tortoise

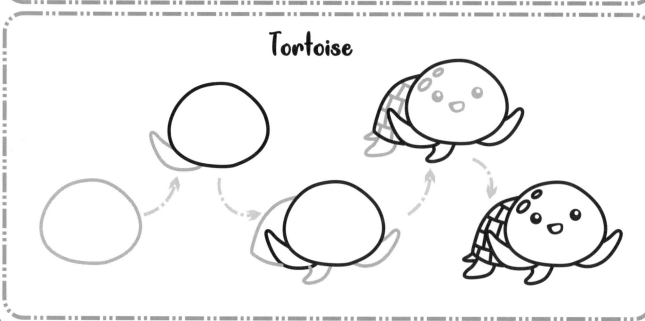

Beet

Hot chocolate

Clock

## Cherry

## Nigiri sushi

## Stone

Ice cream

Mermaid Cat

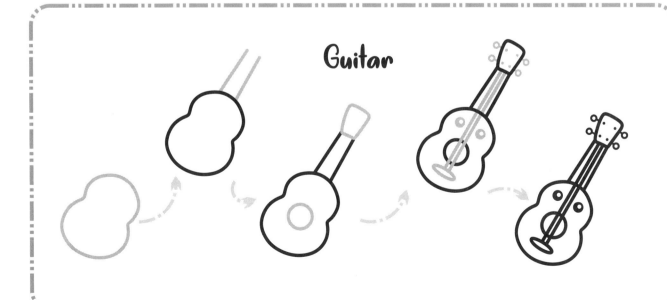

Guitar

Corn

Cinnabon

Sandwich

# Pizza

# Potion bottles

# Laziness

Bread

Candle

Trophy

Bee

French Fries

Scissors

## Stapler

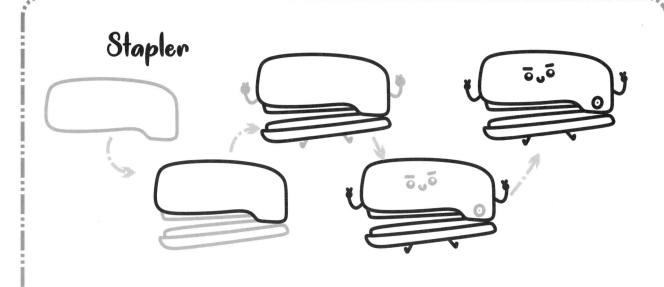

## Lama

## Bathtub

## Sándwich

## Wallet

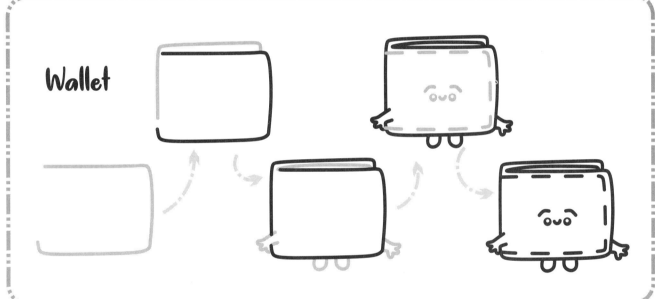

## Egg

Cup

of turnip

Magdalena

**Backpack**

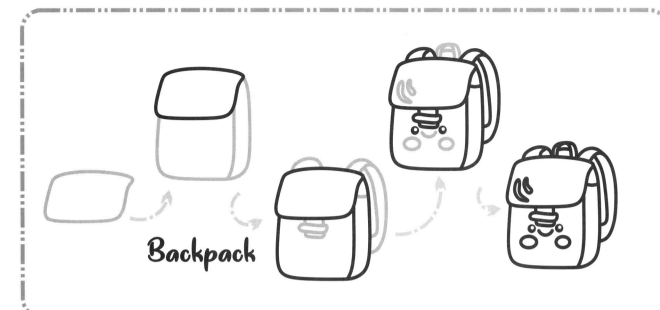

**Sea horse**

**Mermaid tail**

## Pumpkin

## Beet

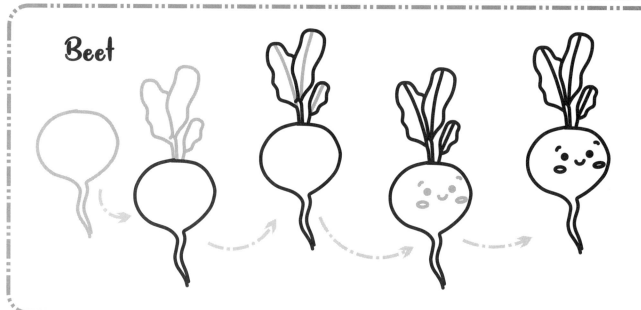

## Kettle

Fungus

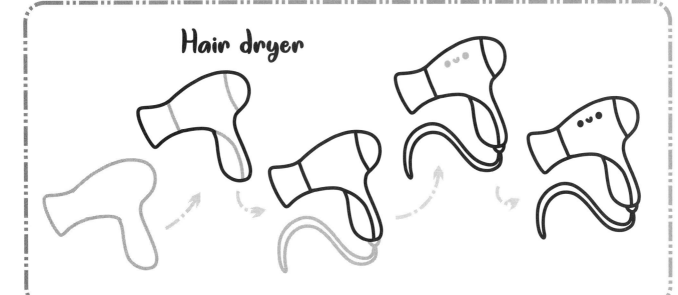

Hair dryer

Pineapple

## Rainbow

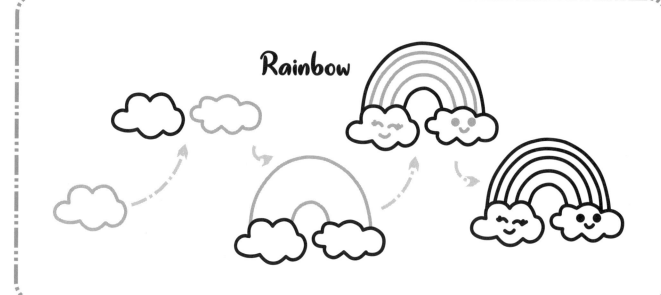

## Cake

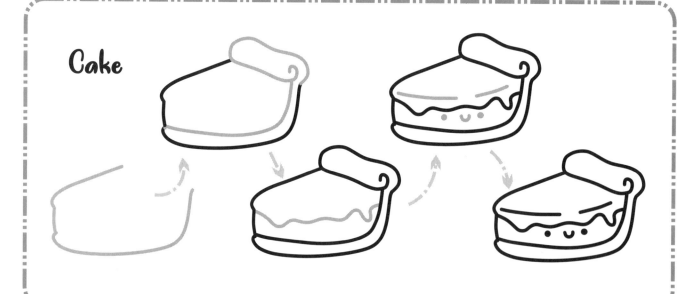

## Spaceship

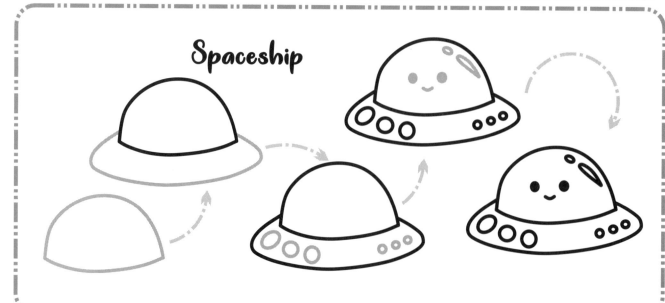

# Milk box

# Draft

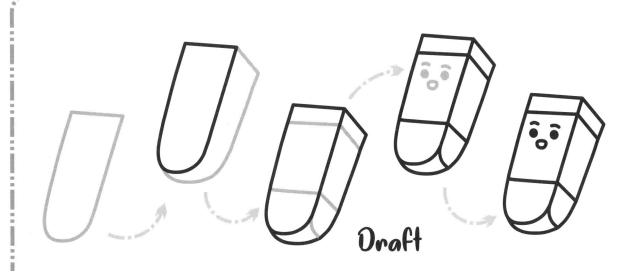

# Platypus

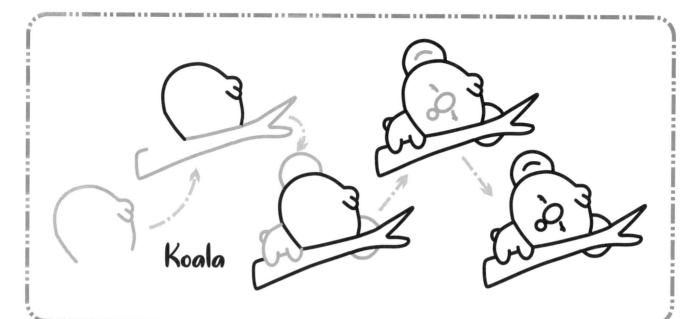

Koala

Teabag

Carrot

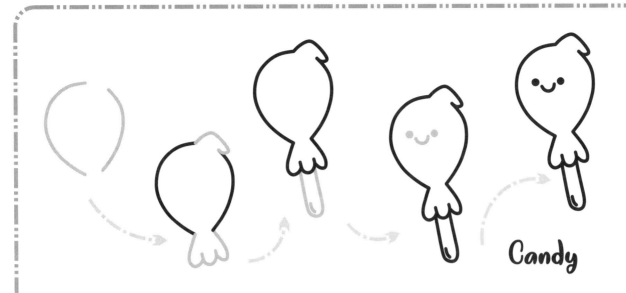

Candy

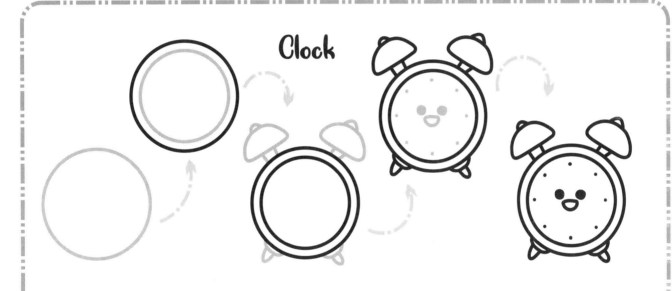

Clock

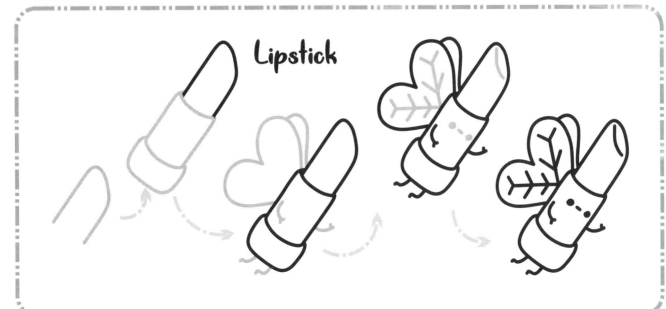

Lipstick

Pliers

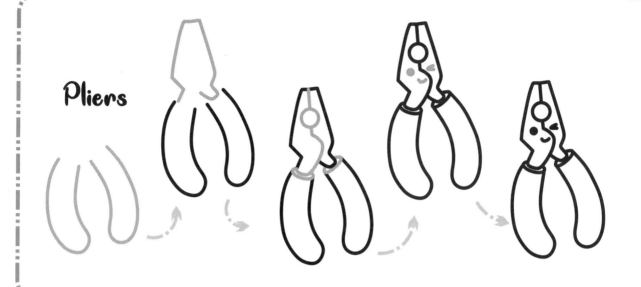

Pig

Giraffe

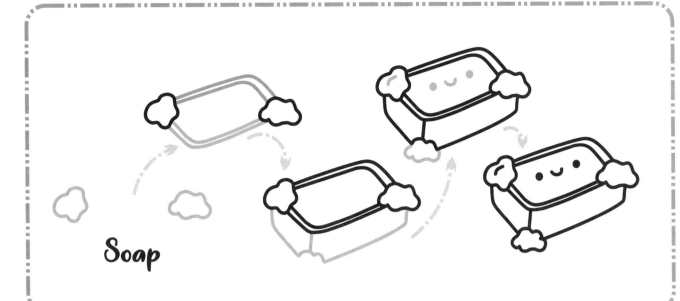

Soap

Fish

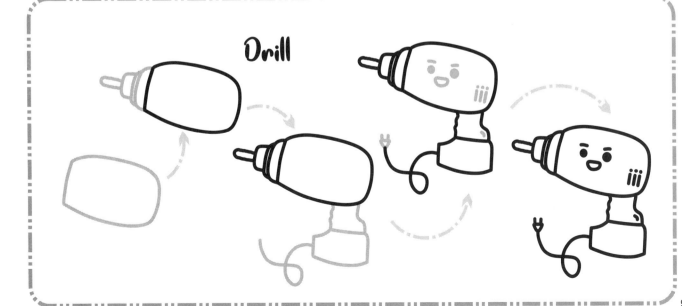

Drill

Rabbit

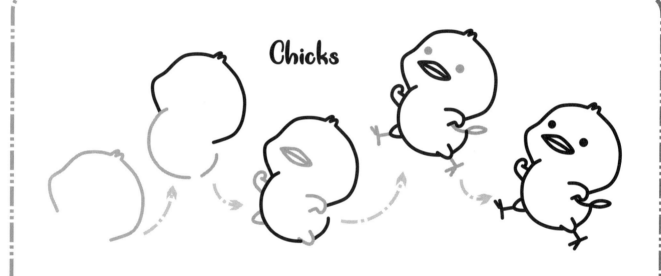

Chicks

Penguin

toothpaste

Book

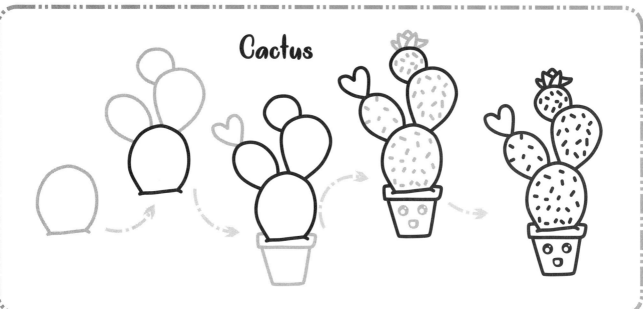

Cactus

## Screwdriver

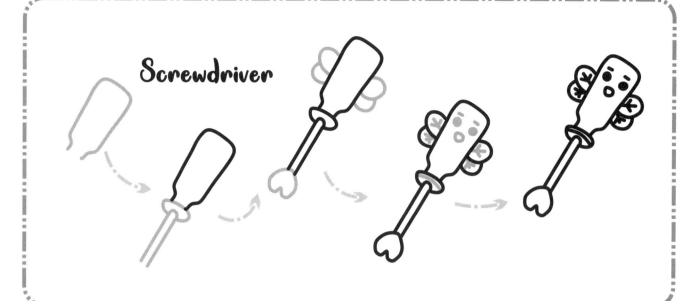

## Sheep

## Bubble

# Unicorn

# Cow

# Dinosaur

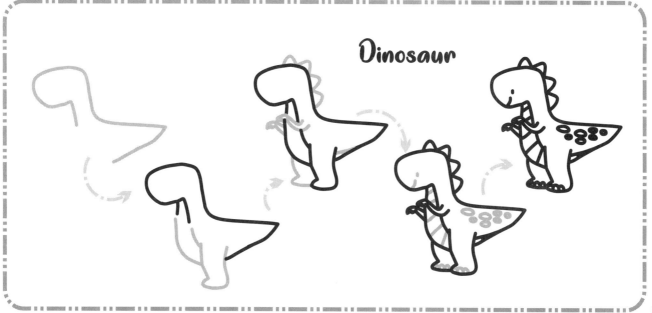

## Hammer

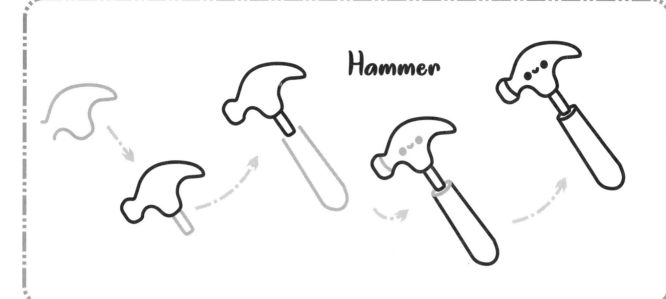

## Octopus

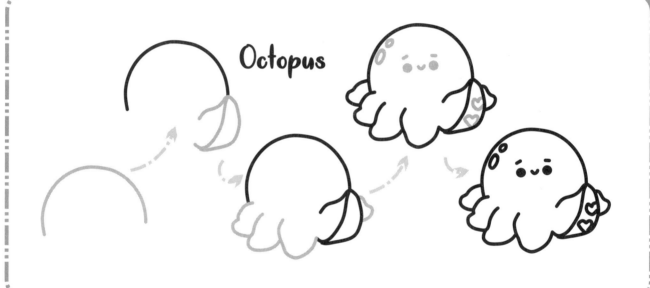

## Plane

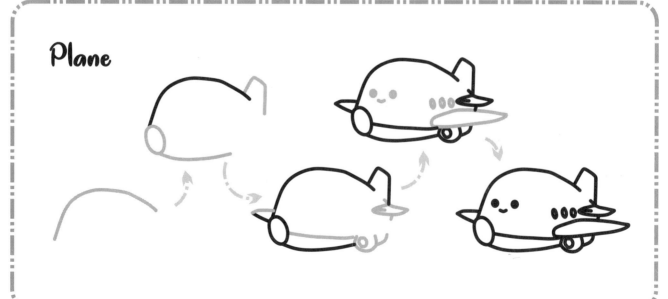

# Owl

# Dango

# Watermelon

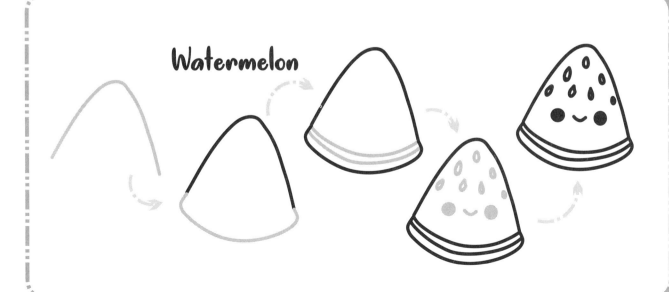

## Shampoo

## Phone

## Sleeping mask

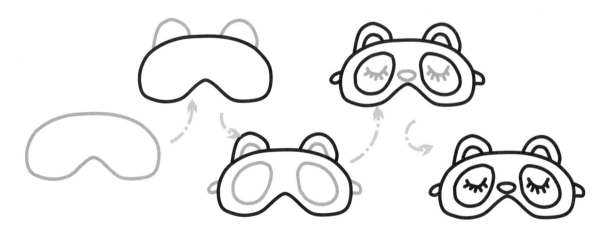

# Bowling

# Siren

# Meat

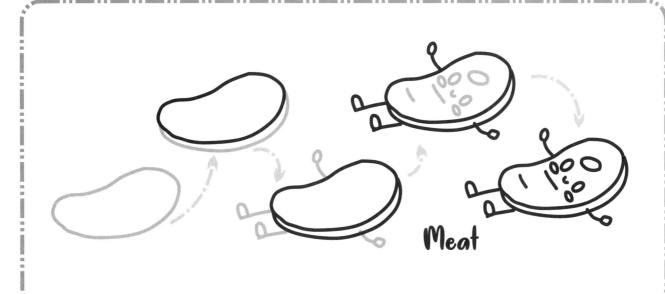

# Easter egg

# Brain

# Skull

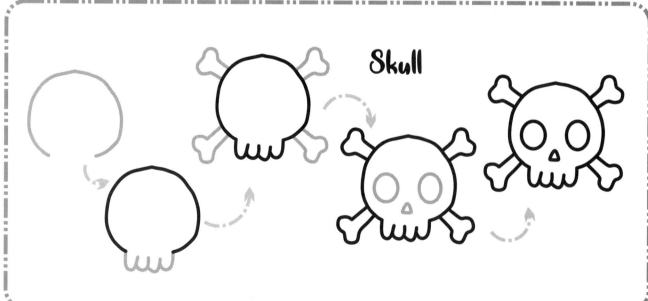

## Ship

## Hot air ballon

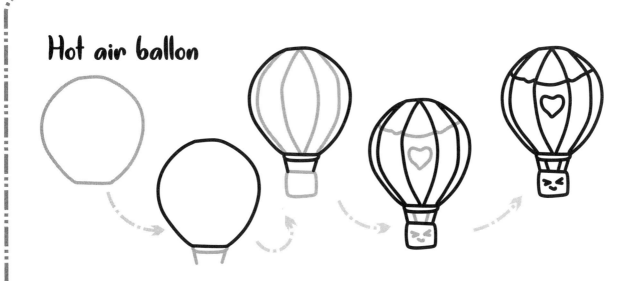

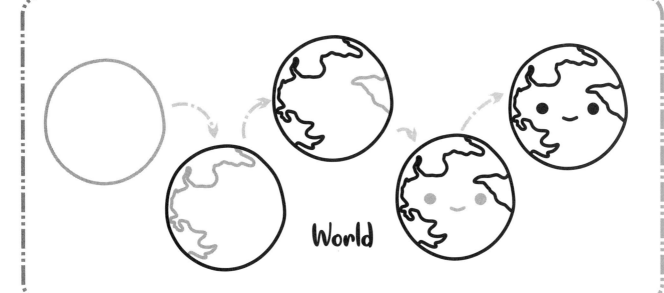

## World

# Papaya

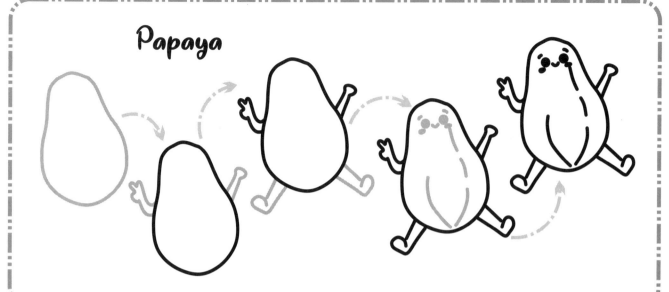

# Rocket

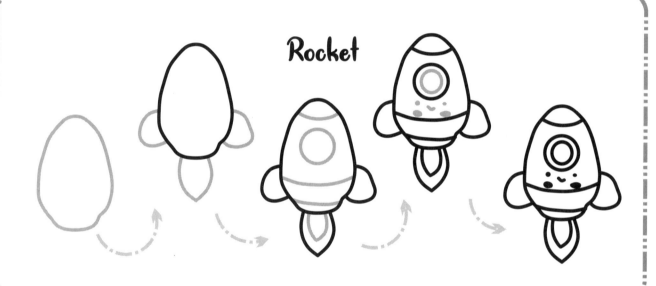

# Dragón

# Eye shadow

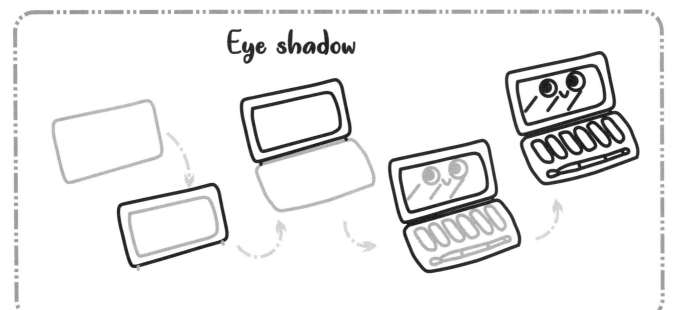

# Crayon

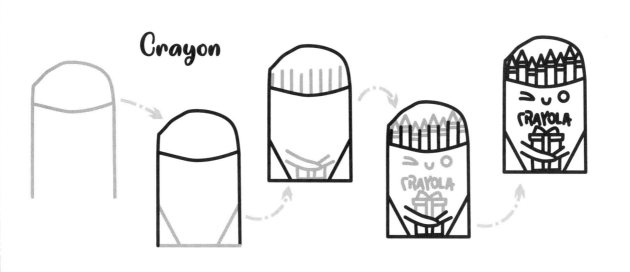

# Grenade

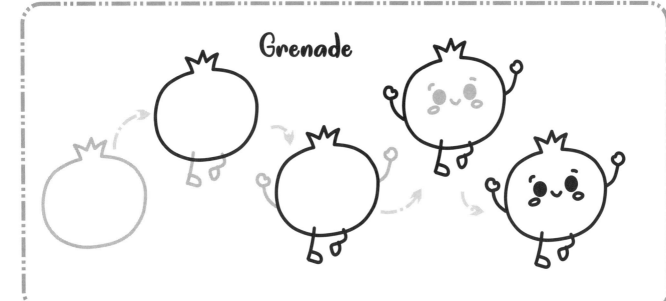

## Insect

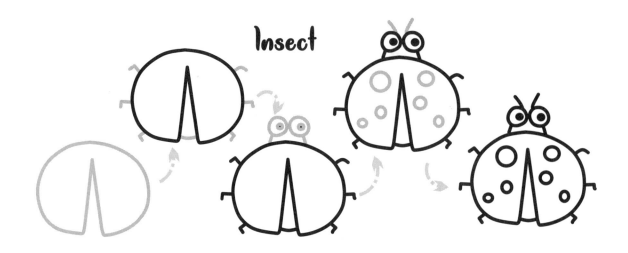

## Coconute

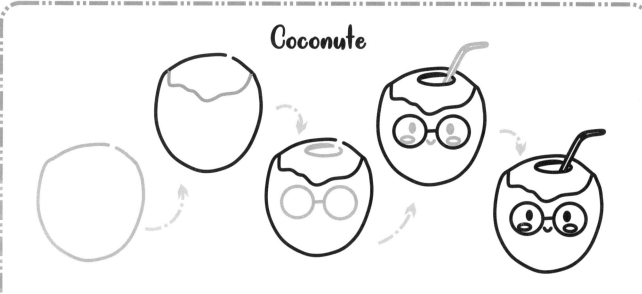

## Magic ball

# Fire

# Glue

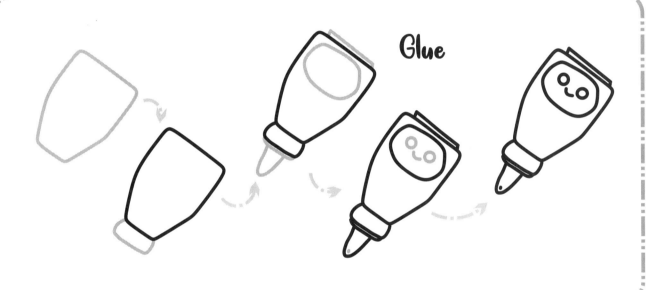

# Marker

# DEAR READER,

I would like to express my heartfelt
gratitude for choosing to bring my anime
drawing book into your creative world.
Your support means the world to me.
I sincerely hope that the techniques
and tips shared on these pages will
inspire your artistic journey
and bring your anime reactions to life
in the most magical way.

Thank you for trusting my guidance.
Happy drawing and may your
imagination reach new heights!

## Best wishes,
## PATRICIA ROGERS